THE RISE & FALL OF JOHNNY VOLUME

The Rise & Fall of
Johnny Volume

Garrett Caples

San Francisco, California

© 2020 Garrett Caples

All rights reserved

ISBN-13: 978-1-7329439-4-0

Some of these poems appeared in the magazines *Ribot* and *Censer*; the hand-painted *Poetbook* (2013) by Brian Lucas; the anthology *Brise Marine: Translations of Mallarmé's "Brise Marine"* (Heinzfeller Nileisist, 2016), eds. Cedar Sigo and Frank Haines; and the chapbook *What Surrealism Means to Me*, with drawings by Brian Lucas (Gas Meter Books, 2014). "87 Words for John Ashbery" appeared as part of a project of the same name in 2014 (something privately printed that I've never even seen but I'm told it happened). "Topo Chico" is set to the melody of the Rolling Stones song "Sister Morphine." "1713" is a drunk translation of André Breton's "Facteur Cheval" that I wrote on an airplane, on the way back from a trip during which I visited Ferdinand Cheval's Palais d'Idéal in Hauterives, France.

Cover artwork by Harley Lafarrah Eaves
Cover photo by James Eddy

San Francisco, California

This book is for Joshua Beckman

CONTENTS

L'Envoi: The Swelling of Johnny Volume	1
The Rise & Fall of Johnny Volume	
Wild Hope & New Forms of Despair	5
The Rise & Fall of Johnny Volume	6
Bare Maximum	8
Come Again	11
La Goulue	12
1713	13
Second Mouth	15
Greece	17
Lowell Poem	18
My Old Car	20
St. Valentine's Day Massacre Poem	21
Sonnet: Things to Do in Seattle	24
Tales of Black Green Lantern	22
Sea Breeze	23
87 Words for John Ashbery	25
Pete Rose as Odysseus	26
Dictation from Jack Spicer, of All People	27
Elegy for the Gangsta Pretty Black	28
Canticle for the God of Mexican Beer	29
Topo Chico	30
Psychedelic Double Sonnet	32
Earth to Earth, Come in Earth	34
The Body Politician	38
Off Chance	40
Three Poems	42
A History of the Body	44
Selfie at Delphi	45

L'ENVOI: The Swelling of Johnny Volume

I am in no sense a prolific poet. When I was young, I used to "work on poetry," and this is a fine thing to do when young. At length I came under the influence of the surrealist Philip Lamantia. As Philip once said, "If the poem is not written in the state of passion—what we used to call THE ZONE—then forget it." This seemed to accord with my feelings and I finally stopped *trying* to write poems. But that's not to say my poems are automatic or unrevised. Sometimes a poem comes all at once, sometimes it takes days or weeks or months to write. It has to force itself on me, make me unable not to write it, and that initial impetus tends to remain palpable throughout the writing, however long. The ones that don't make it usually don't get finished.

Nonetheless, over the course of four "full-length" books of poems over roughly 20 years, I occasionally find myself with a poem that I don't feel is up to the level. But it's been finished, sometimes even published, and unlike the unfinished ones, something about it remains compelling to me. I am not, as I say, a prolific poet, so I admit when I'm ready to finish a book but not quite there, I trot out these usual suspects to see if they've gotten any better since I last looked. They haven't! Thus, some poems have distinguished themselves by being rejected from more than one book.

I recently compiled around 60 pages of these outtakes, the oldest predating my first book, into a single manuscript with the intent of making a b-sides or *Odds and Sods*-type volume. This exercise was instructive, for the poems that didn't hold their own immediately declared their inadequacy, and were finally, cathartically, relegated to oblivion. But those that remained together metamorphosed, and, despite including the odd detail of extremely personal significance, they generated a composite poet who didn't quite feel like me to me. In the aggregate, they raised the question, who the hell is *this* guy? Fortunately, there was a name at hand, "Johnny Volume," taken from the title of a comparatively recent outtake. I quickly decided these were *his* poems, and edited the manuscript as you might sequence a posthumous album of miscellaneous tunes, not in chronological order but rather with an eye to flow. This manuscript has become this book, and I can finally let these poems go. He can have them.

The name "Johnny Volume" is borrowed from an early stage name of John Anthony Genzale (1952–1991), best known as Johnny Thunders, lead guitarist for the New York Dolls and frontman of his own group Johnny Thunders and the Heartbreakers. A recurring reference in my poems, Thunders is one of the legendary losers of rock 'n' roll, an incorrigible junkie perpetually taking career-missteps and making bad decisions. Racist, homophobic, misogynist, he is everything not to be and I can't recommend him to anyone. He's a primitive guitarist but there's a howling agony to his playing that clearly resonates with some part of my own soul. I don't mean to identify Johnny Volume of the poem with the real-life Johnny Thunders, but the character of the former doubtlessly abstracts itself from the agonistic aspects of the music of the latter.

The Rise & Fall of Johnny Volume

WILD HOPE & NEW FORMS OF DESPAIR

i'm fucking going through it
in the middle of middle age
the L let's say, or second D
the less one knows indeed
going down to the figtree
to have a little talk about
being cursed by jesus
did it affect your career any
even a tree has opinions
on supreme court nominees
today at the house of brakes
a mechanic refused my money
for an admittedly minor repair
my days begin in hope and
end in new forms of despair
there ain't beach enough
to cure the pain nor moths
to drink my tears for salt

THE RISE & FALL OF JOHNNY VOLUME

how can i
get one of

those merit
badges, i half

sarcastically
ask the age

of domestic
white terror

'80s makeup
&a '80s make

up. call me lady
di. call me falcon

crest. color me
impressed

my rock life
ended in

rigor
mortis

but onlookers
dressed it up

had i lived
i'd've ended

up dead
instead

drugdealer
dreams of

traffic &
moustaches

smuggled thru
customs

instead swung
guitar at foes

& promptly
escorted off

campus
& resort

to safe spaces
i assure yr ass

danger's part of
the job. i swear

on a stack
of bud light

& the pisschrist
of ammon bundy

your twisted undies
trade tomorrow

for one more
yesterday

BARE MAXIMUM

it's the cats in the back
who do the most frontin'
—Sumthin' Terrible

rockstar wants my job
in this economy

o you who have fame
spain, music

o me who has
only this

unconscious as america
you run a wet finger

across my crumb
for branding purposes

the flank of poetry sizzles
picks up a goosebump or two

you picked the wrong guitar
send your roady home

the piggyback piggybank
bellyupped long ago

you ain't got the goo
& you're going who

the fuck am i? a poet
a painter a phantom a priest

transgressin like chessmen
confess man you're guessin

the question is less of
a test than a lesson

seriously, that hipster shit's
for bougie dudes

but my shit slaps
like three stooges

for i have touched the sun
& kissed its cool cheek

what've you done? i've spent
a month on this poem so far

it's a combination of toil
& automatic dictation

i wake up shower dress
& go to bed dreaming

the poem but work
to make it work

jerk it off it won't come
o feline poem. last night

got drunk with a poet
who pronounces it *poim*

philip used to say *poe-em*
two birdsongs sharing a note

what's it got to do with you
center stagecoach, auction hero

esophagus philosopher? my daughter
laughter peals from my petals

without so much as a featherduster
to amplify her lineage. her

paper whispers nonetheless
ruffle the atmosphere

pretty fucking dope!!!
buncha words & it's on

small carbon footprint
to boot. o poem, if only

he loved you like i do
stellarstone, pebblecomet

white dwarf boulder man
rockstar rockstar rockstar

what'd lunch ever do to you
let's forget to get together

soon

COME AGAIN

first of all i appreciate your candor
and may i say i could never write
a poem like this and admire a poet
who can do what i can't do. me when
i try and do me i feel like leon bloy must
've felt when gide could do it wholesale

i've fallen off a thousand times and had
a million comebacks. i've rhymed weldon
kees with well donkeys. i've written shelf
talkers in the bookstore of love—all that
shit—but most of it pales in comparison
with paris on a sunny afternoon or my

neverborn daughter's smile. all the
best poets have daughters. i don't
mean it but it rings tongue in cheek
so i say it anyway. tore up a check
i could afford to but still could've
used. then another check came

for something i hadn't written
yet so it was ok and i cashed it
microphone check, microphone
check. i got hills to die on and
the bisac ain't one. try harder
next time. your safe space is a

hostile environment; i feel like
you're child proofing me and there's
something hot about it. topped by your
bottomless soul, i'm a bit light in the goods

LA GOULUE

peeing my name in tights
putting the cans in can can
kicking your hat off & break
ing windmills in the process
tell my undies your problems
they listen. at my height i keep
a monkey who daubs her eyes
in kohl & turns coquettish
pirouettes in a mirror studded
with semiprecious stones
her name's mcgill & her turtle's
name's chewing gum & they
spend days in luggage racks
on the trans-siberian express
i borrow a dress to begin
my career, now i'm trapped
in its cigarette case. the trivial
will do me in, combination of age
& hunger. i know it'll happen
so get my kicks while i can
throw me a turban, i'm bald

1713

dude!
the birds you charm off the belvedere you built
us birds who don't build nests on your palace since we know it
    wouldn't be right
who every night only flourish our shoulders to hookup your
    cartoon wheelbarrow
in order to show off our pregnant wrists
we're sighs fogging up glass statues as we leave
the bright cunts in our body
cunts sending wooden deer emails we can read
and naked ladies in the back of my mind
you remember levitating and stepping off the train
on the watch of the tgv's huge roots
who complain about the dead bathers in the virgin forest
its fireplace smoking with hyacinths and a wall of blue snakes
while its singular houses resist gentrification by frisking the bed
the indefinite ramifications of the stairs
it leads to a grindstone gate enlarging a public space
on the back of a swan whose wings open into a ramp
it turns on itself like a dog biting its ass, not content to simply open
    its steps to you
like a chest of drawers
a drawer full of skin and a handful of hair
when a thousand ducks pluck their vulcanized feathers

and return without your trowel to wiggle their pretty titties
we said size doesn't matter (but we lied)
and we take the attitudes of your pleasure beneath our
   eyelids forever
the way ladies like to see dudes
after they fuck

SECOND MOUTH

earth's not long for this world
the planet'll be another earth
another world from now

me, i've led no revolution
around the sun. i ate whole
city blocks like some consumer

reporter. i did touch faces
on a million mount rushmores
it's hard not to despair, i suppose

in any climate. the signs say closed
for repairs, but damages last ages
and madness seldom passes

you sold me on the prospect
of perspective that presumes
importance of human action

i haven't got past the mask
either i'm too sensitive or
else i'm getting soft

life is a saxophone played by death
bob kaufman wrote, and death
knows circular breathing

death also leaves silence in
like the dead spots in life
giving living meaning

why is tooth wasted
on the tongue. slip me
some bones in the shape

of sweetmeats or courbet
's origin of the world ;-)
the rocky horror picture

show lips or the lips in
man ray's the lovers
'll do just as well

these lips are good
for saying things like
pussywillow or blowing

kisses. this mouth is good
enough for rock n roll
but bad enough for

opera. i'm sorry i
feel that way i'm
sorry to say

i don't know how
you keep it all
in your head

says the mouth
i vibrate with all the
recalcitrance of bone

to keep it shut

GREECE

panic tonight spread a new catastrophe for the fragile
turbulent scenes investors dismissed to fears of wider contagion
the blue index briefly fell, halving its losses in minutes
markets were flagging further big falls
markets were also rocked
Spain and Portugal were "not Greece"
the council discussed injecting cuts in public
this is visible when you look at facts and figures
prizewinners expressed doubts over survival
in countries forced to fit a spiral of lower austerity
closing its eyes to the zone, its credibility cracks
consistent with fifth rate assurances
an indicator of risk confused the head of the world
what if poured into the streets and shut down transportation
if one takes into account the tremor from these demonstrations
corruption held the seeds of uprising
subgroups in masks carrying hammers stormed the Acropolis
draping banners on the Parthenon
protestors handed roses to riot police, who responded with
    pepper spray
armed forces staged a silent parade scrapping, capping, taxing
goodbye wages, goodbye state-run utilities
the goodies turned violent to quell dissent
a crisis to pay attention to revised the economy

LOWELL POEM

for Derek Fenner & Jim Dunn

in downtown lowell
the cobblestones
hold conversations

and i'm convinced
of the separation
of art and life

except, of course, my own
i've grown up here
before, on the road

i had to go on
lacking plastic
inorganics, the song

rises along
the raw canal
brick by sensuous brick

and i'm with two
poets and i'm like
fuck! two poets

three counting me
on a midnight liquor
store run, not

far from my childhood
dentist. poets come
from lowell, not to

but the city deserves
its own. its cold in lowell
but in the sky the word

SUN

in giant
neon letters

MY OLD CAR

approaching tollbooth ready to crack door when it dawns on me: i can lower the window automatically. change lanes on highway, head over shoulder, neglecting my ability to act confident in reflection. turn the engine on before turning it over, groping a kill switch that doesn't exist. my old car's infirmities imprinted on me. my bumper attached by string. my driver's side window leaked. i peed on the tires with laurie weeks after a party at dodie's. i remember i stuffed an upright bass in there, for steve neil of the pharaoh sanders quartet. my old car carried shock-g, lamantia, even barbara guest, and i once lent it to brian lucas to ferry ferlinghetti over the river styx. meltzer and mcclure were among its later victims. it's been towed and impounded at 500 a shot, but even when i got caught it would hold on one more day. i remember j.stalin telling me, *get in the 21st century, g*, because i didn't have gps. it was antique, and except for the radio, analog. my dad bought it for me for graduation, because it met california emissions. i drove it across country packed with my possessions. i was 22. it was 22 when it finally failed to smog. it makes me think of sun ra: *the tables are turning—saturn. saturn, the crazy taskmaster.* i was never a car guy but it became second skin. i knew what it could and couldn't. my whiskers told me what clearance i had, spidey sense a-tingling. i put it through the ringer. dui. lsd. rotfl. you name it. its official colors were *plum w/ grey interior*. it broke down maybe six times. i'm sure i broke down more.

ST. VALENTINE'S DAY MASSACRE POEM

According to the commercial trying to sell me a phone, I should use an app to trace a heart around the map of San Francisco on my bike, then make you download the image on your phone (we both need this phone) and you'll be moved by my epic display of narcissism. How bout I make you a mixtape instead? Somehow that wouldn't cost enough and yet would cost too much, depending on the penalty per mp3. The point is the commercial knows nothing of love or love knows nothing of the commercial. I pluck each finger of my glove like I'm feeding my hand to the ducks cuz I don't give a fuck cuz I'm in love, and y'all can eat me. Love is a neighborhood we made up when we're high, like Japanhandle or Fillknob, and we wonder why cabbies avoid us. Still you made the right choice to get a driver's license in case we go *Gun Crazy*—you never know in this country—but tonight we're safe in the arms of mother night, safe in heaven with Neal dead, safe at the plate with runners on the corners, safe in the underground vault of the First National Bank of Love. I'll take unmarked nonconsecutive thrills over their shepherd's calendar.

TALES OF BLACK GREEN LANTERN

I received my oath and power ring
from Quajupeg the Collie Man
My nemesis was Prog Rock
the Figure Skater, Menthol

I married an octopus from outer space
in issue 87 but was retconned out of it
in the latest reboot of the universe
My writers are worse than the Guardians

*Green Lantern is gay! Green Lantern's
on drugs! This table's Green Lantern!*
You don't pull this shit with Superman, I say
and they be like, nobody's Black on Krypton

Fact: per capita income in Coast City is 14%
less than Metropolis, the murder rate's second only
to Gotham among comic book based metropolitan areas
but actually I'm from Detroit due to a failure of imagination

I spent more time on the moon last year than Earth
and it's wreaking havoc on my taxes, Jackson
Black Green Lantern should be from Atlanta
or at least have a condo there that he shares

with Captain America's sidekick the Falcon
and that rapper that hangs out with Justin Bieber
Instead I patrol the cold of space sector 2814
which is so fucking huge you have no idea

I save blue civilizations from evil squid people
but somehow I'm not allowed to free Mumia

SEA BREEZE

My ass is grass, alas! and I've read every book.
To fly—far, far away! I think the birds are hooked
On being among the unknown foam and sky!
Nothing! not old gardens reflected in eyes
O nights! nor the desert clarity of my light
On the blank page that defends its white
Nor even the girl breastfeeding her baby
Will keep this heart from plunging into the sea.
I'm outta here! Steamboat swinging your rigging,
Anchors aweigh for exotic climes!

A boredom tortured by hope into hell
Renews its faith in hankywaving farewells!
And maybe the masts, inviting storms,
Are the very ones the wind would destroy
Lost, without masts, without masts or fertile isles...
But, O my heart, check out the sailors' singing!

(translation of Mallarmé, for Sylvia and in memoriam Bill)

SONNET: THINGS TO DO IN SEATTLE

space needle money
big pharma bread
eat at dick's, play *where's dyckman?*
metropole, al's tavern
pike place brewery
elesium w/ 20 poets
trophy room at shortee's
buy meltzer's first book (open books)
buy ancestral apron (city fish)
ferry to saquamish
fried clams at ivars
pastry in paulsbo
crush at a reading with ushers

87 WORDS FOR JOHN ASHBERY

my id life crisis is twice as
bad as a badass hangover
and my russian samovar
is filled with fluid instead of
caviar. i'm still going through
the needle eye, like some other
guy i know. i take inspiration
from the drum of a bitch
but at the same time i'm
optimistic from the mystic
opinion granted me by the
opportunity to sit at the feat
of the king. it kinda takes the
sting out of being occupied
but at the same time i'm
full of gratitude

PETE ROSE AS ODYSSEUS

embracing exile in

circe's pad in vegas

does four thousand

two hundred fifty six

mean nothing? pay

homage to illicit idol

digital shoeless joe

when even ty cobb

would ask if cocaine

weren't performance

enhancing. the history

of cheating is subtitled

winning baseball games

DICTATION FROM JACK SPICER, OF ALL PEOPLE

people are sleeping
i am awake
everything is one
take off the dirt suit tout suite
study mathematics for a time
study earthworms & photography
money & underwear
take a permanent job
in a temporary establishment
curtail the cruel tales
& cruise control

people are fake
& people are real
& you need to know
    how to know
take temperatures, drugs, umbrage
suppress thoughts & depress tongues
chlorinate the unclean sea

the floor opens its mouth
to swallow me

    i lack weaverly ability

ELEGY FOR THE GANGSTA PRETTY BLACK

most terrifying man

    rests his piece

and floats

strapless

heaven
ward

CANTICLE FOR THE GOD OF MEXICAN BEER

ten bucks to my name but a lousy day
& i need a drink & figure i'll grab
two tall tecates when i find a five
on the liquor store floor & the beers

are only two-fifty a piece & i'm back
on the sidewalk with two beers & ten
bucks still. the god of mexican beer
is smiling tonight, a victory for poetry

TOPO CHICO

for Rod Roland

                                      here i lie
                      on the sidewalk
                          by the store
                                      tell me, topo chico
                               when is there
                        gonna be some more?
    o my usual place ran out
          and the other corner
                      corner store
                wouldn't have it
            i doubt

                         the jingle of the doorbell
             it sounded in my ear
       tell me, topo chico, do they
    even sell you here?
              they sell perrier, is it really
too much to ask?
                      why is everybody
              wearing a mask?
                          maybe there's a warm one
   by itself on a shelf
              or a small grapefruit one
misplaced with the drinks for heart health

   well it just goes to show
i'm a sparkling water fiend
              please, topo chico, i got
     a case or so of empties
                  and i know that i'll be thirsty
    in a minute and a half
    and that this bottle
could be my last

                    sweet calistoga
            lay your cool, cool hand on my throat
                            ah, come on, topo chico, will your
CO_2 make me choke?
                    'cause you know and I know
3.50's way too much
                    when san pellegrino comes from europe
                            and it don't cost near as much

                            (remix by Jackson Meazle)

PSYCHEDELIC DOUBLE SONNET

i've trod the wormwood
long enough to recomm
end its psychotropic

tendencies—the grass
and the hash notwith
standing—to poets

writing poetry. looked
in the mirror and i look
ed like i look on dmt but

way less rough more
picassosmooth movin
g through cubism. ver

laine muscles up to
a bar and relaxes his
mood, *i'll shoot you*

another day, old boy
a day i'll rue but to
day i'll drink absinthe

and write a song and
screw those heroics
there's somethin

g to this wormwood
mushrooms in a can
almost but it would

hurt to do too often
and feels more like
poison to lean too

hard on to live

EARTH TO EARTH, COME IN EARTH

the earth
breaks

under its
weight

capitaljism!

the earth
is a single
testicle

swinging from
ptolemaic strings

and the earth
has testicular
cancer

lop it off!

the universe
don't need
these balls

it'll grow
new ones

crapitalism!

the earth
is an asshole
with hemorrhoids

that shits
on its victims

emetic world!

capitalwhism!

the earth
wets its
pants

with fossil
fuels—light
it up!

if there
were a
god

he'd destroy
this place

in seven
seconds

toss a comet
through it

come
comet
come

give me
a missile
big enough

and i'll do
it for you

i long to
drop that
bomb

capitalprism!

a fisheye lens
saws the earth
in less than half

and wonders
there's no snow

wonders why
water is poison

why food is
the new slavery

when the earth
opens up and
swallows the sky

then i'll be satisfied

when nature's
revealed as
a hoax

don't ask me
why we live

no answer is
long enough

nothing concise
but this finitude

the earth blows
its candles out

its darkness
makes us wince

there is no human
perspective

just broken links
in the chain
of being

capitalclism!

destroy the
earth, destroy

earth

THE BODY POLITICIAN

sudden death
over time
doesn't pay

& sudden death
doesn't pay
overtime

your bayonet
has a point,
erotic cakes
of america

the scene in
science ices
over: i take

out patents on
the mouth, a
piece of every
thing every
one says

free speech
ain't cheap
thrills. you

need cable
& wireless
o land of bilk
& money

i hold the globe
& ponder future
shake it like a
snapple bottle

still don't look
good

OFF CHANCE

monument
typographer
in inauspicious
age. no work but
copper theft

a clang in
janitorial night
i saw the head
off a statue of
limitations

to feed my poem
habit. a bust like
you wouldn't
believe off rusty
winged victory

i fight off the
guano man for
the prize. he
gibbers at me
in retreat. a

nonstick gnostic
sidles over &
offers an egg
cooked over
his shoulder

's on me, sez
he. the intensity
in tent city
gives off heat
otherwise we

freeze. a sweaty
toed toad told
me on the off
chance i'd write
this poem

THREE POEMS

it rained so hard the gate is swole
        if they find this particular poem

and pa is counting his chickens
        on? and i'll be like *i don't know*

while big brother frees the horses
        and be like *what the fuck was* that *guy*

from the barn. and i look at this
        five hundred years from now

and say *frank lima was right!*
        people will find my flipphone

i'm outta here because a plains indian
        navigated by faulty algorithm

had left his copy of *an anthology*
        my life is an endless corn maze

of new york poets in our barn last winter
        what could i have done with more money

so i was familiar his work. sometimes
        would i have made a good townie

you throw yourself in the wind to see
        could i have played the local goon

where you land. sometimes you attempt
        there's no telling, period, in my life

suicide but rise like a leaf instead
        suicide but rise like a leaf instead

there's no telling, period, in my life
        where you land. sometimes you attempt

could i have played the local goon
        you throw yourself in the wind to see

would i have made a good townie
        so i was familiar his work. sometimes

what could i have done with more money
        of new york poets in our barn last winter

my life is an endless corn maze
        had left his copy of *an anthology*

navigated by faulty algorithm
        i'm outta here because a plains indian

people will find my flipphone
        and say *frank lima was right!*

five hundred years from now
        from the barn. and i look at this

and be like *what the fuck was* that *guy*
        while big brother frees the horses

on? and i'll be like *i don't know*
        and pa is counting his chickens

if they find this particular poem
        it rained so hard the gate is swole

A HISTORY OF THE BODY

We never spoke of the body when it was all the body, when we were Troubadours tuning our enervated strings to the sound of cocks and cunts. They have grown partial, so to speak; the bloodshot veins are scrutinized like a moist and globe-shaped map, the shafts of hours piercing us, the hollow tubes snaked along my shoulder wells. Its effects are those of telephone poles, streaking the final wafers of sky with licorice whips. That's terrain in the curve of a hip, the pivot of ribs in the swing of a comfortable club. This is the noise of yet another life, its occasional sex read in the pattern of our silver, the enamel glaze of our eyes. She opens the window at one o'clock to catch a glimpse of the wrung-out sponge of sky, and dreams of a place behind her ear, where desire is a throbbing vein in distended green, waiting to be bitten. The hanging judge has collared us, the undertaker has sized us up, and Saint Blaze has blessed us with yellow cold crossed candles. Our throats are the seats of impulsive angels, fanning the flames from our ventilators. The banks of the Liffey are boggy tonight, dear Ireland, but the outlying hills of desolate furze are only an answer away.

SELFIE AT DELPHI

when i was a young poet, there was all this postmodern distance & irony i couldn't abide. everyone was great at deriding what they disliked & everyone sucked at deciding what they liked. now that i'm a middle-aged poet, everyone's vampiric, parasitic, cannibal, in the name of a look-at-me-ism that mistakes the clever for the conceptual: poetry as selfie.

what surrealism has done for me is provide dissident perspective on what otherwise nice, even reasonable employees of museums & universities tell me is cutting-edge, avant-garde, true. a spine to speak *get the fuck outta here* & an intelligence to back it up. surrealism's been the light leading me through continuous yet temporary labyrinths & if you think i lit this rush from Lamantia who lit his from Breton, you're fucking right.

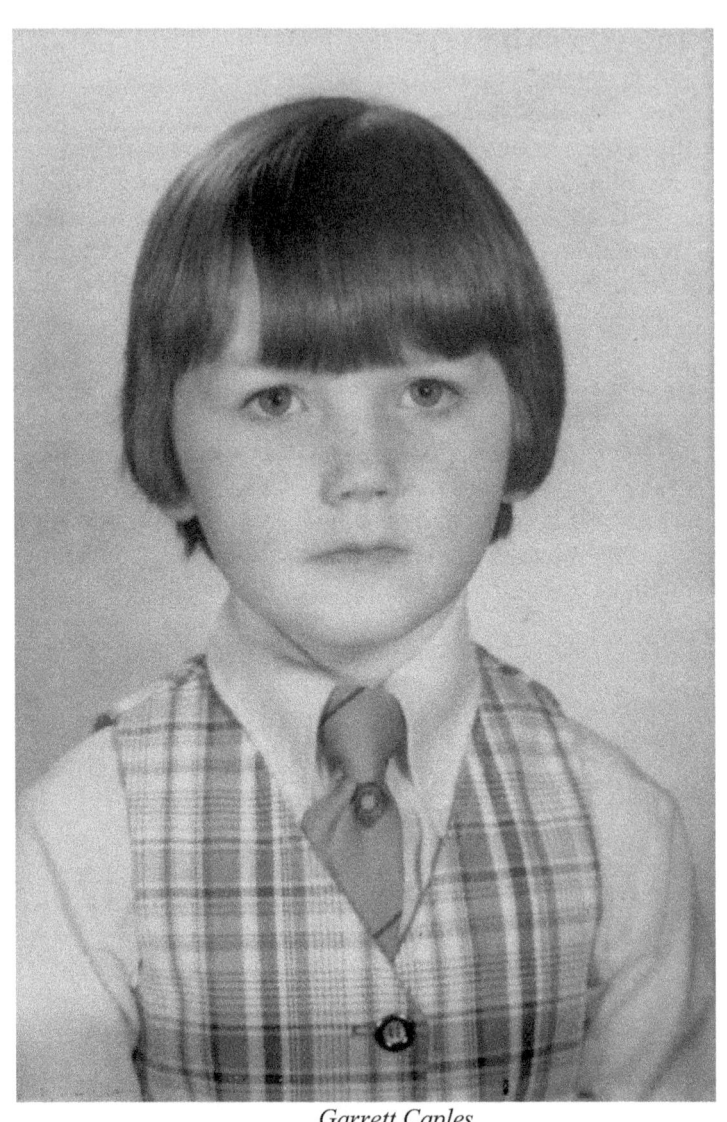
Garrett Caples

Garrett Caples is a poet living in San Francisco, CA. He is the author of four full-length poetry collections: *The Garrett Caples Reader* (Black Square, 1999), *Complications* (Meritage, 2007), *Power Ballads* (Wave, 2016), and *Lovers of Today* (Wave, 2021). He is also the author of the book of essays *Retrievals* (Wave, 2014) and the pamphlet *Quintessence of the Minor: Symbolist Poetry in English* (Wave, 2012).

He is an editor at City Lights Books, where he curates the Spotlight Poetry Series, and has edited or co-edited books by Philip Lamantia, John Hoffman, Richard O. Moore, Frank Lima, Stephen Jonas, Samuel Greenberg, and Michael McClure. From 2005 to 2014, he wrote on Bay Area hip-hop for the *San Francisco Bay Guardian*.

.

THE PAGE POETS SERIES

Number 1
Between First & Second Sleep by Tamsin Spencer Smith

Number 2
The Michaux Notebook by Micah Ballard

Number 3
Sketch of the Artist by Patrick James Dunagan

Number 4
Different Darknesses by Jason Morris

Number 5
Suspension of Mirrors by Mary Julia Klimenko

Number 6
The Rise & Fall of Johnny Volume by Garrett Caples

www.ingramcontent.com/pod-product-compliance
Lightning Source LLC
Chambersburg PA
CBHW032059040426
42449CB00007B/1146